Author's No

This book features 100 influential and inspiring quotes by Conor McGregor. Undoubtedly, this collection will give you a huge boost of inspiration.

1

"The more you seek the uncomfortable, the more you will become comfortable."

2

"Life is about growing and improving and getting better."

3

"My success isn't a result of arrogance – it's a result of belief."

4

"I'm not going to get somewhere and say, 'OK, I'm done.' Success is never final; I'll just keep on going. The same way as failure never being fatal. Just keep going. I'm going to the stars and then past them."

5

"You might win some, you might lose some. But you go in, you challenge yourself, you become a better man, a better individual, a better fighter."

6

"I wish everyone well, but you need to focus on yourself. You need to stop putting your hand out. Everyone wants hand outs. Everyone wants things for free. You've got to put in the work. And You've got to grind. You've got go through the struggle, and you've got to get it."

7

"I'm just trying to be myself. I'm not trying to be anyone else."

8

"I enjoy competition. I enjoy challenges. If a challenge is in front of me and it appeals to me, I will go ahead and conquer it."

9

"I'm just a kid that defied the odds. And I'm just a kid that ignored the doubt. I'm just a kid from a little place in Dublin, Ireland, that went all the way, and I'm going to continue to go all the way."

10

"My family's lineage, we are warriors. The McGregor clan, we are warriors all through. We are famous all through the world for our fighting capabilities of all generations. So I have no doubt that's stood to me and that led me down this path and gave me what I have."

11

"Nobody is my boss."

12

"To do anything to a high level,
it has to be total obsession."

13

"I don't feel pressure in a negative way. And I like pressure. I feel excitement and calm at the same time. No pressure, no diamonds. I want pressure: pressure creates drama, creates emotion."

14

"People think I'm a celebrity.
I'm not a celebrity."

15

"When I am free to train and free to move, I feel like a gorilla in the jungle. Then, when there are a bunch of media obligations, I feel like I have been captured and am being kept on display."

16

"My preparation is about precision. It is a science."

17

"We're the only animal that wakes up and doesn't stretch."

18

"I guess I have a little bit of an ego. I'm confidently cocky, you might say."

19

"I take inspiration from everyone and everything. I'm inspired by current champions, former champions, true competitors, people dedicated to their dream, hard workers, dreamers, believers, achievers."

20

"I am fearless."

21

"Life's a rollercoaster. You're up one minute; you're down one minute. But who doesn't like rollercoasters?"

22

"I believe in believing. My coach John Kavanagh is a big atheist, and he is always trying to persuade people to his way of thinking, and I think, 'What a waste of energy.' If people want to believe in this god or that god, that's fine by me; believe away. But I think we can be our own gods. I believe in myself."

23

"I run New York City!"

24

"If you deserve it, go get it."

25

"When I say something's going to happen, it's going to happen."

26

"I'm interested in movement, and I'm interested in money, and I'm interested in the movement of money"

27

"The thing about the truth is,
not a lot of people can handle it."

28

"Ritual is another word for fear,
manifested in a different way."

29

"Yes, sir, no, sir, clock in, clock out. Why were you late? Why are you not in today? That's not how humans are supposed to live."

30

"I am in the fighting game. And I don't care about anything else. I don't watch the news, I don't care about politics, I don't care about other sports. And I don't care about anything I don't need to care about. This is my sport: it is my life. I study it; I think about it all the time. Nothing else matters."

31

"Posture for combat is so vital."

32

"Trash talk? Smack talk? This is an American term that makes me laugh. I simply speak the truth. I'm an Irish man."

33

"Why go through life if you're not going to challenge yourself?"

34

"I'm just looking to learn, grow, stay focused, and become a better fighter and a better athlete."

35

"I train and I go home, and when I'm home, I think about training. That's my life every day, and that's it."

36

"My dream is to be World Lightweight Champion in the UFC. Have more money than I know what to do with. And have a great life for my kids, grandkids, and everyone in my family."

37

"A good feeling for me is when you train, and then you put on fresh clothes. New clothes after a training session – you have this rush of endorphins from exercise that everybody gets, and then you get that nice feeling of fresh clothes. It's a double whammy."

38

"If you are surrounded by your competition and you are outworking these people, outmaneuvering these people, it's hard not to let your confidence take over. It just builds and builds and builds."

39

"I used to pretend that my Peugeot driving to the gym in the rain in Dublin was a Ferrari on the Vegas strip."

40

"I carry the flag of Ireland all the time. I want to represent my country."

41

"I certainly would not like to end up in a tie-up with Ms. Rousey."

42

"I'm in the game of spinning plates. And I'm spinning a boxing plate. I'm spinning a Tae Kwon Do plate. And I'm spinning a Jujitsu plate. I'm spinning a freestyle wrestling plate. And I'm spinning a karate plate. If I was to put all them down and have one boxing plate spinning, it would be like a load off my shoulders."

43

"What it's like to be me? You know, it's good to be me. My life is good."

44

"I always teach myself calm and
visualization stuff."

45

"I've read a lot of books on the laws of attraction, and in my home, I have a big book on Muhammad Ali, which I've read because he is, like, a hero of mine, but other than that, no, I'm not a big reader."

46

"My goal is to be number one in MMA."

47

"Some people take defeat and losses a certain way. You see how some fighters take losses."

48

"I don't look at a man who's expert in one area as a specialist. I look at him as a rookie in ten other areas."

49

"It's good to make your brain
work more than your body."

50

"I love money because I've earned it. I won sixty G's with my first knockout – and the week before, I was collecting social welfare."

51

"I think it's an Irish thing. We don't really care. We say it as we mean it, and you have to deal with it. The truth is the truth"

52

"Competition gives me energy.
It keeps me focused."

53

"There's people that tried to celebrate when I lost that got nothing to do with it. That's not the sign of a champion."

54

"People like to blame others. I think a person should just look at their own situation, look around them, find out what they wish to do, and seek and go and do that. And that's it."

55

"A lot of people cry and complain and put their hand out and beg. It never goes well."

56

"I want to be an expert in different fighting styles, new training methods, new ways of thinking."

57

"I don't feel bitterness, I don't feel anger towards anybody. Fighting is never emotional to me."

58

"I'm focusing on me. I'm focusing on my family's security, my family's financial security, so that's all I can do."

59

"My unpredictability is what separates me. If you move in so many ways, your opponent is not focused on what he's doing. He's focusing in on what you're doing, and it freezes him. When they freeze and you hit, they shatter like glass."

60

"From the moment I open my eyes, I'm trying to free my body. I'm trying to get looser, more flexible, to gain control. Movement is medicine to me."

61

"I just figured out that if I gave my all into this game – if I put everything into the fight business – then I would eventually run the fight business."

62

"Boxing is limited fighting with a specific rule set. Fighting is true, where you can do anything."

63

"The left paw has done me well over the years. I'm not a scientist, I'm a martial artist."

64

"I am not afraid of saying something and going and pursuing it. That's it. I see it in my mind. And I say it out loud. I go and do it."

65

"This guy's a clown! He's just all talk!' I've heard that many times in my career. And then they're sleeping in the middle of the octagon."

66

"I break orbital bones."

67

"When I prepare, I am not messing around. I find the right places, the right people, and the right environment. Iceland is one of those places."

68

"The only time my records are going to be broken is by my own spawn. I'm going be training that child out the womb."

69

"I'm already the face of the UFC, plus the face of boxing, WWE, and Hollywood."

70

"Everything I've been thinking, every vision, even down to every shot I throw, it just ends up here in reality. Whether it was in a fight and how to react or whether it was in a stadium with screaming fans or whether I was in a fancy car or the best clothes ever, I always put myself somewhere."

71

"I always put myself out there. I'm not afraid to commit to something."

72

"At 155, I will be the same animal, an even better animal."

73

"I have a deep, deep belief that if I tell you I'm going to crack you with a clean shot to the chin inside one minute of the first round and you will be unconscious, well, then that's what will happen."

74

"I'm committed to the fight game."

75

"If I hit a man, his head is gonna
go into the bleachers."

76

"I never got into training to be an All-Ireland boxing champ or to win a belt. At the start, I just got into it to learn how to defend myself when I got into situations."

"People think hard sparring will get you sharp. And you do get sharp in the gym. But anytime I've trained that way, I've actually been a little bit flatter in the fight. And the knockout shot hasn't come. It's almost because my training has been too hard."

78

"I've always felt like there was a lot of hype around me even when there wasn't. I felt like everyone was talking about me even when no one was talking about me."

79

"Not a lot of people or pros in this game know how to train correctly. That's why they don't have a long career. Their body gets banged up. They get into a rhythm of heavy sparring and heavy work, but through that, they're limiting movement."

80

"I'd love to go into WWE and have a real knock and see what's what."

81

"There's many ups and downs in the fight game."

82

"It could be if I fight in front of one person or one million people. It's still the same emotions."

83

"Any top-level athlete, it's always the same. There's always that hint of arrogance there... It's hard to be humble when you're the best."

84

"I'm going to change the way martial arts is viewed. And I'm going to change the game. I'm going to change the way people approach fighting.

85

"Yeah, the Mac Life... it's about sipping some tea, getting together with the knitting circle. You know I like origami, right? That's how you get to be notorious."

86

"I want to negotiate what I'm worth. I want to put my analytics forward, man-to-man, and to be like, 'This is what I'm owed now. Pay me.' And then we can talk."

87

"I see fighters make funny videos about me and stick them on Facebook and get 20 likes. When I make a video, I sell it to Fox and make seven figures. That's the difference."

88

"Many people don't understand ring control. They think they do until they're against someone who really understands how to set traps, how to create holes in the octagon that they fall into."

89

"I don't fight in chase of an individual. And I hear this sometimes where fighters work their whole careers to reach a matchup with a certain individual. I do not think in that way."

90

"I think I am the greatest fighter in any class. I know I can hold two, maybe even three belts."

91

"I am not stupid. And I am a very bright guy. I know that in the fighting game, you get people who get brain damage and do themselves long-term harm."

92

"I have the greatest job in the world. I get paid loads of cash for beating the crap out of people. And I'm very good at it."

93

"You beat him verbally. You beat him mentally, and then finally, you beat him physically. That's the three ways to beat a man."

"People say that I'm a boxer. I actually started with kick boxing, and then I moved onto boxing, and then I moved onto grappling."

95

"Glutes are power."

96

"I've learned new footwork patterns that are very unusual. I've learned how to find a lower centre of gravity, and I've found more angles to throw shots."

97

"Cage Warriors is a brilliant organisation. They're doing great things for European MMA, and they're giving the platform for guys like me who came through. They're vital. I'm forever grateful for the opportunities I got."

98

"You might be tough, but you can only be so tough for so long, you know what I mean? The brain can only take so much damage. The body can only take so much damage."

99

"That's what I do this for, to secure my family's future. I don't care about anything else. I'm able to spoil people, and that's the best thing."

100

"What can I say? I'm a talker."

Printed in Great Britain
by Amazon

36836020R00056